I CAN HEAR YOU, CAN YOU HEAR ME?

NOLAN NATASHA

Invisible Publishing

Halifax & Picton

Text copyright © Nolan Natasha, 2019

All rights reserved. No part of this publication may be reproduced or transmitted in any form, by any method, without the prior written consent of the publisher, except by a reviewer, who may use brief excerpts in a review, or, in the case of photocopying in Canada, a licence from Access Copyright.

Library and Archives Canada Cataloguing in Publication

Title: I can hear you, can you hear me? / Nolan Natasha.

Names: Nolan Natasha, 1982- author.

Description: Poems

Identifiers: Canadiana (print) 20190156724 | Canadiana (ebook) 20190156732 | ISBN 9781988784380

(softcover) | ISBN 9781988784427 (HTML)

Classification: LCC PS8627.O65 I23 2019 | DDC C811/.6—dc23

Edited by Anne Simpson
Cover and interior design by Megan Fildes | Typeset in Laurentian
With thanks to type designer Rod McDonald

Printed and bound in Canada

Invisible Publishing | Halifax & Picton
www.invisiblepublishing.com

We acknowledge the support of the Canada Council for the Arts and the Ontario Arts Council.

*This book is dedicated to
Tucker Finn*

SIGNALS
Walkie-talkie 1
Thanksgiving 2
30 4
New radio 5
Relax, you said 7
Rental car 8
Fidelity 9
Queer 10
Mirror 13
A boat sitting in the forest 14
Women's studies 16
Lightning on the road 17

SOUVENIRS
I miss you 21
Fishing 22
Forks of the Credit River 23
Handmade box 25
First game 28
In between 30
Niagara Falls 31
Getting married 32
Divining 34
Montreal 35

PHENOMENA
Sighting 39
National park homo 41
Arachnophobia 42

Sisters · 47
Mountain updrafts · 48
Sideways snow · 49
Not having a dick · 50
My body, full scrape · 51
Inherent · 52
Love song · 53
Trust · 54
Christmas at Point Pleasant · 55
The moon! The moon! · 56
Anatomy · 57
Waterfowl · 58

DEVOTIONS
Controller B · 61
Sailor · 62
Batting practice · 63
Snow day · 64
Homesick: Toronto · 65
From God · 66
February · 67
Lovers · 68
Not knowing · 69
Faith · 70
Gestures · 72
Revelation · 73
Cognition · 74
Celebration · 75
Girlhood · 76

SIGNALS

Walkie-talkie

I can hear you, can you hear me?
I can hear you,

can you hear me? The running family joke—
that's all you ever wind up saying
into a walkie-talkie:

I can hear you, can you hear me?

You on the back end of Hollyberry Trail,
me rounding Applegate Crescent,
throwing my bike to the ground,
hiding from nothing behind a hedge.

I can hear you, can you hear me?
Roger. What's your ten?

Apple thirty-six over. The code. Heavy metallic tangle
of a tossed bicycle. The crouching,
the fact that you are blocks away,
one hand on your handlebars,
pulling the antenna up with your teeth.
All of it.

I can hear you—

Thanksgiving

    The only picture of us was taken from far away.
I had just changed my name and the whole world seemed
    as new as us—a few weeks.

    Hungover every morning
in your bright pink room,

the white curtains dulling the sun   only slightly,
   your cat mumbling
      until I got up and filled his bowl.

  When I came back to bed,
his small mouth crunching from the kitchen,
      your face soft and creased.

Nowhere to rush to for the first time, we had dinner plans,
but during the day—

      we slept late,
      drank coffee,
    and had sex in all your chairs.

The food that night was the most delicious I have ever eaten.
    I don't mean this flippantly.
Course after course and—
    I don't remember what we ate. Not really.

Turkey, obviously,   and stuffing   and some kind of a mash—
I know I kept saying—*Oh my god! Oh my god!*

And I don't know how,
    but I know that the next morning—after walking home
from your apartment
              my body humming through the cool air
                      and grind of the streetcars

the bundles of newspapers waiting on doorsteps
       somehow

                the sound of her voice—
on my answering machine   taking it all back—
       her apology
waiting there for me
       pulled me backwards—

      made me misplace what had happened with you.

Made me put it in a category of things
       that will happen often to me.

Of things I thought would happen often.

30

All the teenagers I talk to have never
heard of *Reality Bites*.   No, it's a film.   Oh.

      I eat more Kraft Dinner than is safe, I'm sure, but
I have trouble letting go.

We used to sit on the back deck and pour Tabasco,
the red and the green, onto the glowing
orange heaps in our bowls.   You'd smoke cigarettes,
I'd play records through the window,
and we'd both yell about what was broken

and what was beginning.   One time, Erika was there—
she came back after the bar, drunk and hungry.
She had never tried it with the green Tabasco—
and this felt like getting somewhere.

      The easiest thing is to miss someone. To repeat yourself.
The noodles are perfect in seven minutes—
you can count on this.

Purple Rain was on the stereo.
One of the kids asked who it was.
It's Prince.   Oh. I like it.   Is it new?
No. It's not new.

New radio

Her clothes folded in neat piles on the bookshelf,
except the ones she had just been wearing

                                            jeans hunched

on the radiator, tank top on the desk
covering a sketchbook and an overturned copy
of *Even Cowgirls Get the Blues*.   Her armpits,
lush with rebellion.   Above the alarm clock, written
on the wall in Sharpie, were the words

                                              CUNT POWER.
  This was the highest I would ever look up to anyone.
I had nothing figured and was sure of everything:
I think punk rock is stupid.   It's just noise.   I could do it.

                                                I'm sure you could.

She got off the bed. It creaked   and felt bigger.
She took a Bikini Kill CD off the shelf, tossed me
the liner notes and pressed play.

                                    I'm going to go take a shower.

                       She grabbed her towel and left.
The disc played out—
        nine short bursts.
Voice like a megaphone
with a pinched nerve.

I sunk lower and lower, shins dangling
from the mattress, neck bent toward tossed and sweaty sheets.

Drums slamming out of the small tinny speakers
      into the walls of her six-by-ten room
           where everything happened for the first time—
loud, but not as loud as it could have been.
                        Not as loud as I wanted it.

When it was over, I could still feel the wailing voice
                        in my teeth.
I got up, looked out over a crisp layer of snow on the rooftops
and tree branches above couples
      dropping each other's hands
            as they stepped off Church Street.
All the white glowing yellow and orange from the lights of
                        the city.
      The music kicked open a door
and the room felt—   bigger.
The view, different too, warmer—   hot, even.
      The air inside and out—
damp.

      She came back still wet
in just the towel.   Smiling.
She loved me.   She knew what she'd done
                      and said nothing.

Relax, you said

Sound advice, but you said
many things, all week. Your
voice. The trees. Birds we can't name.
You said, *How are you feeling?*
And I told about the flu moving
through my body, but never
answering. *How are you
feeling?* Like I'm falling. Perfect.
My eyelids glued together
with morning mucus, but I managed
to get them open before you
arrive, so—no matter. You said,
Did you sleep okay? No. I'll likely never
sleep again, I thought, looking away
and watching you watch me take a sip
of my coffee, your reflection next to mine
in the window. All week, you said many things.
But that night in my bed, your soft arms
reaching, glasses not yet on the nightstand,
my body, clothed and taut, you said,
Relax. It wasn't a suggestion.
Laughing, as though you hadn't
just changed everything. All that worry, left
in the sheets behind me, as I turned
to face you.

Rental car

Under the hood, belts run their course.   Each piece
of metal with its own   gravity.

      Beth always said
you used to be able to fix a car with a roll of duct tape.
But now   it's all too complicated.

      Winter tires hold us, just barely,
to this world, this monochrome day.
      White road, white sky cut
by black, trees and rivers,   crows leaving familiar branches.
White gathered on limbs,
      clumped and heavy, like our voices. My jacket tossed
in the backseat where we aren't.   We aren't
   tuning forks,   but the hum of our bodies,
filling this rented air, transmitting us out
      into some collapsing orbit.
Say handsome one more time,   I dare you.

How long does it take to make a canyon?
    That's how hard your questions will be to answer, later—
in the still of my hotel room. The car parked outside.
    Not going anywhere.
                    Not going anywhere.

Fidelity

I look up the root of the word
platonic. If you were here I could simply ask.

The next day I found ways to say your name
to the server and to Catherine.

I mentioned you to my coffee cup several times,
and the pines, but not the birch,

because that felt like taking things too far.

It's not just that it means one thing
written in heavy books
from the university press and another in your mouth
as an answer and another on the stall door and another
hurled from a car on that Saturday in the spring,
on posters that grip telephone poles
promising a good party—

it's something that argues with its own construction,
restless and glistening and grimy,
takes issue with the sentences of this poem.

In that bar on Queen Street, words and little pictures
etched by greasy fingers in the red plastic coating
on the candles. Drawings, obscene
and tender decorating the dark tables,
flickering into the establishment turned
home. The living room of our twenties and thirties.
We will dance and be sick,
sweat and stumble into each other's vacancies.

The way our bathrooms feel dirty is different
than the bars with the big-screen TVs—soccer piss
and sweat is not the same.
Does this recital filter down to our bodily fluids,
or is there some smoke and mirrors
that causes his hands, but not his, to feel that way on my hips?
I am asking this sincerely.
Does the air only feel this way
because of some lesson in breathing?

Because of some lesson in breathing?
does the air only feel this way
I am asking this sincerely.
That causes his hands, but not his, to feel that way on my hips?
Or is there some smoke and mirrors,
does this recital filter down to our bodily fluids,
and sweat is not the same.
Than the bars with the big-screen TVs—soccer piss
the way our bathrooms feel dirty is different,

sweat and stumble into each other's vacancies.
We will dance and be sick,
home. The living room of our twenties and thirties.
Flickering into the establishment turned
and tender decorating the dark tables.
On the candles. Drawings, obscene,
etched by greasy fingers in the red plastic coating
in that bar on Queen Street, words and little pictures

takes issue with the sentences of this poem.
Restless and glistening and grimy.
It's something that argues with its own construction.

Promising a good party—
on posters that grip telephone poles
hurled from a car on that Saturday in the spring,
as an answer and another on the stall door and another
from the university press and another in your mouth
written in heavy books—
it's not just that it means one thing.

Mirror

Geese squawk through the phone.
In the park two blocks from your apartment
you move from bench to bench, try
to stay warm, your hands take turns
in the cold, holding your cellphone.
The hours pass this way.
We say and don't say. The wind dances
each strand of your hair in infinite combinations.
The geese laugh and occasionally
so do you. I leap between these moments
as if I'm crossing a river—
wet stones and twisted ankles. I hear
the wind in your ventricles, the howling wonder
thickening your blood. Hope rises and sets
with the light. Look into the pond and see me,
staring back from the bottom, through your
reflected eyes. The geese brawl; we say *I love you*
and it echoes through what's left of November.

itting in the forest

 years, it has come to look more and more like a rock.
There is no way to know what the deer think.

> *I would have never known if you hadn't told me.*

I think this is meant to be some kind of reassurance.
        Invisibility.
Deep voice, broad shoulders,
                I've had the mannerisms down for years.
The trick is to look at the eyes. The eyes don't change.

I meet expectations now and am lost in the trees.
                              If there are words
for what this feels like exactly, I don't know them.

> *You look like you. You sound like you.*

Their relief is as unsettling as their discomfort.
It is the same thing.

> *You must feel so good.*

The little things—
morning face in the mirror, a single thin white T-shirt
                        on a hot day,

swimming. I breathe easier—more.
My body is heavy. It knows where to go.

Mostly, it is the space
to see outside, that nothing is fixed—only closer, different.

Women's studies

    Hours pass in the lecture hall of our beds.
  My armpit, your left shoulder. On camera,
all of Quebec between us,
    we'll talk about how my stitches, and the wounds
they clench, dissolve in your gaze. But first,
        let's get the orgasms out of the way, clear our heads.

Later, you'll read my shame and make an offering—
put it just so—like no one has:
That's not what that feminism is for, Nolan.
        And I even believe
  the things you see when you look at me,
my bare chest backlit by the lamp, your eyes scorched
with wanting.
      The man I have become,
the girl I was   long ago   jumping from the swing set
landing with both feet in the gravel   firm.
                I was really there,
  a kind of knowing.
            You make it feel like that again,
easy to trust what is plain. We are who we are,
    mountains hold power, and the geese are beautiful.

Lightning on the road

Cracks in the sky, grey
of my stomach. Possible ulcer,

pace of the wipers, my clamouring
all these months, since the first time

I heard it in your voice:
sudden illuminations. Nothing

is as we imagine. On this New Brunswick
highway, the rain slowing us

dangerously, hazards flashing.
You'll ask if you can call me tonight

in my hotel room, the phone buzzing
the way it does just before lighting strikes.

SOUVENIRS

I miss you

the way one misses a country. All the minutiae
of a place. The designs of the candy bar
wrappers. The texture of the jokes. The shape
of the sidewalk stones. I can live without
your arms for now, but soon the taste
of your tattoo ink will gather in the inlets
of my mouth. I will weep, sorry about
the deep breaths I took in your absence, slip
on my shoes and think of the cracked soles
of your rubber boots—how you kept
wearing them, your soggy feet bringing me home
daisies with the spare change.

Fishing

It isn't what it used to be.
My uncle hooking the worms, pulling
the fishes off. All the sick parts,
punctured flesh in his hands.
Me casting out, reeling in—

>   repeat
>   repeat
>   repeat   *phhsss, dwuit*, tug, reel, tug, reel.

He caught less than I did. Baiting the hook, driving the boat,
answering my questions.   Why do things float?
The relationship between mass and volume. My small chest
hugged by bright hot orange—plastic buckles, bare feet

on the cool aluminum,
  looking down at the green rocks undulating
as spade-shaped ghosts sailed between—waiting. For fish,
for the darkening sky. Just one more cast, then another,
  till dusk,
with its weight, and the smell of gasoline, pushing us back

to the lamps inside the cottage windows, back to the green
leather sofa and grandmother in the home stretch
of her novel, a box of chocolates tucked under her pillow,
the creak of old mattress springs.

Forks of the Credit River

We used to twist my car around the river
off Highway 10. Way, way up,

chunky planks of the train bridge,
running,

broken ankles in my mind.
Stand By Me—

it feels like the movies in this valley.
The daring of being young

I never had. Never
jumping,

always holding. Twisting
around the same river,

its bank, romantic.
Our feet in the water,

Tom and Huck—
a couple of girls.

I could tell you anything,
even the time I lied

about getting punched in the face
to keep her from leaving.

That maple bent over,
its fingers dragging in the water.

Our feet in the river,
jeans rolled, handsome—

a couple of girls.

Handmade box

Numbered highways stitched
across Ontario fields—
                         the grid of Toronto
                                 expanding into wheat,
corn, and dead sunflowers.
                      That little blue car,
you driving on the right side for the first time,
                                    tense and attentive,
             but laughing
             and turning to me
as often as you checked the mirrors.

     Parked on the gravel shoulder, we walked
up a trail that appeared to head into thick forest   but opened
     into a field—   a vast strip cut through the trees
and a footpath worn through the tall grass.

The void made the opposite woods appear
                like an island in a dry golden sea,
            waves around us standing still—
        matted blades paused mid crash.
We left a faint wake in the calm air as we walked—
                    you in front of me.

      The opposite woods were darker
in the valley, the trunks of the poplars stretched,
     trying to outreach one another.
Under our feet small bits of wood and leaves—

     you pulled me to the ground, or you must have,
        because we ended up there—

catching my breath, I noticed the mischief on your face,
    that it had been there all day.

    The trees, their bare branches, a black web above us—
    what seemed like thousands of arm lengths away,
as far as the sky,
part of it somehow.

    I took a picture looking up,
    cranked the film, stretched
my arms like the poplars
    and turned the camera back down at our faces—

your black black hair,
the sharp edge of your bangs,
that striped sweater, so soft
         it would look out of focus in the photographs.

      Months later, on my eighteenth birthday,
you were as far away as you could be—
halfway around.   We joked
                on the phone
                      about digging a tunnel.

A handmade box arrived in the mail
filled with feathers and gifts the size of card decks.

    That day's sky glued to the inside lid

and our faces on the bottom, 4x6, looking up.

    Inside the box,
    the web of thin black branches
    and white grey sky
               above us still.

First game

All day at the Ex, ride after ride,
my father and brother saying,
We have a surprise for you!

Cotton candy and my first corn dog.
Seasick funhouse floors. Metal carts grinding
through buzzes and sudden lights
of the haunted mansion. A few missed tosses.
Fishing a winner from the duck pond and the limp-armed teen
assuming I'd want the Barbie. Young

enough that the grit on the heaving machines
didn't show between the lights and the kiddie rides
still soared majestically. The sun dropping

behind my brother, my dad's hand on his pocket.
Their goofy faces beaming,
> *Are you ready?*
And my father revealed three thin strips,
raised them in the air,
> Blue Jays tickets.

The cable cars were still strung up over the grounds
and we sailed towards Exhibition Stadium, the three of us,
with a bag of small warm donuts. The smell of cinnamon
and sunscreen.

The ball players were tiny sailboats sliding
across the green. Sitting beside the scoreboard,
I watched the golden-orange bulbs
  collect into the figure of a pitcher
winding up and firing.
  The whole day's exhilaration turned to sand
in my thin body. By the fourth inning, I was curled up
in my blue plastic chair. The Jays won, but by that time
I was long gone—eyes shut in left field.

In between

Stumbling from your birthday party,
I smell like sausages and wood smoke,
and the night is far away from my body.
The sky is only strips, ribbons of smooth ceiling
above the alleyways. Between these garage doors,
to work and home, to work and home, in right angles,
always dark—booze on either end.

I'm going home to feed the cat, grab a sweater.
I'll meet you back on the patio
and wonder what I'm feeling about you
and your hooded sweatshirt and your hands like paws.
You'll sit across from me, beside the curly hair
of your girlfriend, and she will be witty
and tell me I'm too earnest and I will like her
as much as you—in a way—my intentions irrelevant,
because I'll be too drunk by then, I might be now,
everyone will be. That's how it goes—
that's what we're all doing for the time being.

Niagara Falls

I was driving, you took over the stereo. That Lucinda song
I'd never heard. Lodestar too. We ate bad pizza.
You beat me at Skee-ball. We must have looked at the falls—
I remember how nervous you were at the blackjack table.
How I learned you are afraid of heights, handsome
in any T-shirt. How I dared you to charm the girl
at the prize counter, just so I could watch you—
I held your hand, wanted to take your arm.

It is almost impossible to imagine you then,
  in that tacky motel,
not yet my partner, no longer my friend, so newly
my lover. The roar of the water—even when you don't hear it,
it pours and pours, erasing the rock underneath.

Getting married

Everyone is getting married. Everyone is getting married
and I am aware of feeling annoyed—

different. You and me in that ruined mill
where people in denim with rough hands worked

before it was a provincial park. Before I went there
on a Grade Ten field trip to learn about glaciers carving

potholes into the bedrock, before I climbed
out of the yellow bus, stretched my legs and decided—

that was the place. Before I walked between the sagging walls
with my clipboard and pencil and on the little bridge inside—

the perfect place to stand, half-moon above the small river
that used to power the mill's wooden machines—

years before I brought you there, before I tricked you
into staying, if it rained we'd just hand out umbrellas

to the crowd. Before we had the idea about the lanterns—
how the guests would set them on the water,

their names lit up and floating.
Before I asked you.

And before the night two weeks later when we agreed
we were far too young, clinking the necks of our bottles—

our whole lives ahead of us.

Divining

Just when you think you know the colour
of the sky, you see the way it talks

to the mountain and then there are more
shades of grey and blue in the windshield than stones

in the sea. And you realize you know
nothing and that knowing is nothing,

that naming the colours is good craft,
but futile because you can't even say

what you feel. And you can touch the gear shift,
but not her leg, so you look at the colours,

say, *Wow! Look at that! Isn't that something else?*
And she tries to name the colours too

and does much better than you. But because
you aren't listening as hard as you're breathing,

you won't remember what she said, but
you will still see the colours and you will still feel

your hand that is not on her leg.

Montreal

All the signs in all the windows
that read—*for rent*—in French, seem,
at first glance, to say—*a lover*.

We came for a summer weekend.
The first of many
rooms where we would cry
into each other's bodies. Where
her tongue, fisted, would beat words
into my body until the Greyhound
took me back to Toronto. Bloody,
I used to lick my arms and legs
on these streets. But now

I dip my bagel in the hummus. Admire
the shoes. Wonder whether espresso
is masculine or feminine. Grateful
I have someone else to ask.

PHENOMENA

Sighting

The stars were not what kept us there, or the glowing
that appeared below Cassiopeia, waving veins of light

in our direction. No thick black sky crawling with stars
could've kept me on the roof of the boathouse—

a mansion for spiders. But I lay on the cold shingles
and so did you—touching. Just.

Tucked in my arm eventually for warmth. August chill,
everyone else inside, on the couch, or the spiral of the rug,

bottles in hand and eyes closed. On the pullout,
he was asleep, looking like a fawn,

tattooed like a rock star. If I believed it was a UFO,
it was only so I didn't have to get up.

I'm not sure we're looking at the same thing, staring
down your arm at one sliver of the sky. *There. Right there.*

Later, in the kitchen, we leaned back against the countertop,
drank red wine and played with that old dictionary.

Opening it with our eyes closed and pointing:
You are   a hamadryad. You are   the Niagara River.

You told me about your sister, marked my height on the wall
with the rest. Our teeth stained with guilt,

the morning peering through the window, you asked—
Why do you write about the things you do?

I don't remember what I said,
only the way the light fell on your collarbone.

National park homo

Stand in the window in your underwear,
trace the mountaintops with your gaze.
What is the wildness you feel you are
in this place?

What is your strangeness? Ask
the deer moving through the trees.
Try not to lose your breath. People
will look, but they will not see you.

You are more magpie
than you realize. More hidden too,
like the big cats,
their yawning desire—

look at the mountains.
It is so easy not to.

Arachnophobia

When I saw you fall from the shower curtain, I thought about
calling my new friend—asking her to take you away.
    Usually Lou does this for me. Or Adam from upstairs—

    but I am far from home
and I was naked when I found you—
        afraid
by the time I got dressed you might have hidden.

So, when you crawled to the bottom of the curtain
and it was easy to knock you to the floor,

        I killed you with a sneaker
                              and I'm sorry.

When I was five and you were in the corner, up high,
                              I would wait
before calling my dad
        and think,

    Nothing will happen, nothing will happen,
        nothing will happen

if I leave you alone.
                              But I wasn't brave
    and by the time I was ten,
my dad had bunched you up dozens of times
  in wads of toilet paper.

My uncle used to tease me about you—
                              then he lifted the BBQ cover
                            and you were there hunched,
                      the size of a mandarin orange,
            and he saw me standing
           in the middle of the yard for hours,
           not touching anything, or looking anywhere,
                    until someone could drive me home.

    After that, he read a book about fear
that said we should put you in a jar and name you.
                And I didn't have to look at you,
            but I always had to say hello and goodbye.

I have never flipped through *National Geographic*,
as I suspect you are sometimes photographed.

    I thought I would never go anywhere warm.
But when Emma asked me to come home to Australia with her,
                I was so in love
                      I didn't even think of you
            for five whole minutes.

I tried to prepare—went to the zoo, where you are the biggest.
        Twenty minutes to walk down your hallway, another ten
                                        to lift my head.
        The wall beside you said you could eat birds.

I went outside, collapsed on the snow and cried.
                                    I was so proud.

  Above the telephone table in our house in Perth,
                          you were the size of a dish rag.
  Beth, in her denim vest, was the only one brave enough.
      With a rolled-up newspaper, it took almost a full minute
              of beating you into the hard wood.

I got my plane ticket out of the drawer.   But I stayed
and we tried the trick with the jar again.
                          I called you Julian.
Because I like the name
and it made me imagine you wearing an argyle sweater.

Hello, Julian. Goodbye, Julian. Hello, Julian. Goodbye, Julian.

  For the first time, I wanted to look at you and did.
  Soon, I was camping in the desert, under the stars—
      no tent, and I assume you were there too.
                                    I felt strong.

Jumping from the dock that day,
    turning back in the water and seeing you hanging—
  near the ladder,
              black and thick.

All I remember was Lou's panic on the shore,
        throwing me a life jacket, begging me to stay calm.
    Cliffs on either side,
  the ladder was the only way out of the water,
    and some part of me would rather sink
    than swim towards you.

People say about you:

It is more afraid of you than you are of it.

                                          No.

It can't hurt you.

                              I nearly drowned.

On the fourth floor of a building downtown,
  I learn about trauma
    in one-hour appointments. For some
        it is the way your legs move. Like hands creeping—
the idea you could be anywhere. Amygdala too sensitive.
                Memories compressed
    and focused in my body and yours.

I'm afraid you will touch me. I'm afraid you will touch me.
                              I'm afraid
    you will touch me.

I'm trying to change this—
even at your most robust, you are so very small
                                and I am so
                                much
                                bigger.

        I know something about this
        and I'm sorry.

Sisters

The evening was parked. Still.
We sat at the edge of the cliff throwing sticks
and stones at the water. She said—
>*You already make sense the way you are.*

Across the water there was lightning. We stood
and watched iron clouds gather in the still air.
One moment it was all so far away
and the next it turned to face us,
the wind running at us, only us.
The sky was warm, sweet, and held out
as long as it could before wetting the cliffside
and forcing us under cover.
Later, in the orange-black of the tent, she said—
>*Maybe it's because you're my sister*
>*and the word means something to me.*

Our bandanas were stained
and bunched together with sweat.
The sky that morning paid no attention
to the night's storm.
What's done is done.

Mountain updrafts

Do you want me to leave? you asked
in the dry heat of my hotel room. Unable to speak,
I unplugged the alarm clock and you smiled.
When air hits the mountain, there's nowhere to go
but up. That morning we prayed for a storm, something
to ground you. I will try to keep you in small ways.
Read the words you've written. Eat at our table
by the window. The clock still unplugged.
I regret not looking at you in the forest.
Instead, eyes peeled for wildlife,
feeling like prey. Leaves rustling
with impermanence. We are not supposed to say,
but this was love between us.

I've been baptized by mountain updrafts. My name
new in this air and your mouth. Those short days—
the road obscured by snow. I didn't know
where we were going, but I wanted to show you
the canyon. Drive closer to the monuments
that had been watching us. Take you out
from under the failed ways we had named this.

Sideways snow

Tiny white birds,
their congregation everywhere
in the blue-black sky. I imagine
their joy. A vial of testosterone and sesame
oil in my palm, where the curves
of your skin just were—

in the cave of our minds, a bag of cherry blossoms.
The soft ivory of this snow. I tell you
I want you.
        You have me,
you say again, stepping off another bus,
my feet in spring now. The thickness of your words—
the flakes, tracking past. Your voice
caught in the net of my mouth.
I am almost home. You are almost
home. We are almost home. Almost.

Not having a dick

But I do. The thing is
I'd forgotten how to think about
that kind of wanting. Then you asked me:
    What would we do, if we were going to touch?
Just like that
the truth of my body—
every slight move. The way
your hair would fall across your
left eye, my right hand there
to meet it—your calf against
my palm, the way you looked
a bit afraid when I finally
kissed you.
The way you
penetrate me
so deeply.

My body coming home to a fire
after trudging through snow.

My body, full scrape

across this pavement
toward you.
      The tide drags us
out before it flows back
into the bay,   fullness
between distant cliffs.
Cut of water carving
islands out of rock,
      your body,
its weight beside me
in sheets. Coffee in paper
cups and my whistling
in the morning as I bike
past the park—its flatness
under the dogs
and children. Coffee
in paper cups, Sunday,
and God is wondering
where we are—hoping
we've figured it all out
by tomorrow when he
opens his eyes, lets thunder
fall out of his mouth
like laughter.

Inherent

My hand on your thigh, running up towards
your centre. The gravity of this, the sinking
mattress. This rhythm, this wanting, cellular,
coded in drips of DNA back and back and back
to the beginning. Ages before I declined to shake
your hand, meet your lips. And then as if called
by all the needles on all the pines, green slivers,
infinite pinpoint pushes forward, I tipped—
spilling over you. My hand, your hip, our mouths
opening and closing as if to speak. Ask
for a way in. Down the hill, people are talking
about their daughters and sons, husbands
and wives. They are pulling clothes from the dryer.
Calling the cat inside. Finishing the wine. I push
myself into you as if nothing else matters.

Love song

A knot at my centre
has been untied. For better or worse

this will not be held in, lashed to the cleat,
no. We think of the horizon,

flatness stretching in either direction,
the straight edge of the sky, sharp

against ground, water. But what
of the mountains? The city? What horizon?

What does one thing have to do with another?

Trust

A new feeling: tectonic plates
shift under the couch,
the bathroom floor still dirty—
but we aren't fighting about
those kinds of things anymore.
How could we? How could I?
Questions caught like hair
in the food. Your generous face
wants only the most
simple thing: to be alone
with me. Finally, we stopped
holding our breath and let
the bats fly out of our mouths,
fill the room, hang, like us,
above the bed. But this morning
the ceiling was just a blank page,
like the first time I woke up
in your bed. The whiteness
of your sheets, behind your curls—
the thickness of your hands.
All that potential.

Christmas at Point Pleasant

A white day, we took a walk
after the presents. It was before
the dog, just us two. We turned
into that small clearing at the top
of the path. The part I always said
was my favourite.

We ducked into the trees like
teenagers in a stairwell, hiding
their kisses. We stood still
as the chickadee flew
back and forth, back and forth.
A tiny unwrapped gift.

I won't tell you about this year,
how in the brown and green I stood,
left the dog at home, waited
for the chickadee, wanted
to see its small weight
like hope on the branches. Cursed
every absent snowflake.

The moon! The moon!

I'm learning to fish but I'm too afraid
of the entrails to eat. Please come back.

I'll light the fire, pour the wine.
Toast the one sweatshirt you left in the hamper.

The moon is full, but I'm not sure
why we care.

Yes, miraculous!
The tide! The water inside us,

but what about the blackness, the sliver moon?
How it shows so plainly our shape—round

against its body. Come down to the water.
I'm learning to fish—

open the belly, pull out the guts. Think of how good
the mackerel will taste.

I want to sit with you. Spiders
under our chairs.

Anatomy

When your hands
are back in Ontario
parts of me will vanish—
pipes of my heart, the places
my body manages
to reach outside itself
towards you.

Tell me I'm really here

while I look at the new leaves
on the fingers of the birch,
how impossible the green
would be without
the sun.

Waterfowl

You narrate for me the goings on. Mallards, geese,
a single swan. The ugly suburbs of Ontario. A vegan
café your only respite—but I don't want to be right
that Kitchener is a shithole.

That swan gets all the attention because
people are idiots.   Baby, how many times
do I have to tell you, I don't know which waitress
you're talking about? I was in formation, flying with purpose.
Was I taught this pattern, or is it in my blood? Stop
acting so surprised I called back to you from my
throat. You talk about our wings like they're hypothetical.
A hawk circled and now you want
to learn its taxa, markings, habits, so next time
you'll recognize

                        what is happening,   but darling
I'm not sure there is a next time

                                what is happening.
Tell me again about the geese—how they find a lover,
eat the grass, complain about the children in the park.
                        How do they feel
about each other? Tell me again
                        what is happening.

DEVOTIONS

Controller B

Our Nintendo never died. Eventually
the screen started to flash solid white
and orange. All the kids knew
how to fix this: take the game out
and blow into the cartridge. Blow hard
along the whole edge like a harmonica.
Tilt and lower your head
so you face the console.
Blow into the back of the machine—
mouth to mouth.

Now I hope—with my adult
lungs—I could make Mario
drop from the sky again,
if I plugged in the console
and breathed into it.

Sailor

I doubt there could be anything
as delightful as drinking whiskey from your dimples,
but I haven't done it yet.

I looked down at the planes tattooed on your forearm
and wanted to know what kind of sheets were on your bed.

Over eggs, you rolled up your blue sleeves and told me
about a boat back in Nova Scotia.
                              So you're basically a sailor?
Yes, you lied.

A week or two later,
  you tapped the bend in my shoulder and said,
It's time to get up, porkchop.

The word   porkchop   caught
in my stomach—an impulse
stalled and spun,

spun for years, in tighter and tighter circles.
I held my breath, leaning away,
until there was nothing left to do but let go

and yell, *Marry me! Marry me!*
across the water.

Batting practice

I spent more time in the back field than any other place.
Tossing the ball up gently with my right—
swinging through with both hands.
     Sometimes Andrew would come outside with his glove
and catch the ball as it fell from the sky.
     Wish my little sister could hit like that, he'd say.
But mostly I would stand alone,
  watch them like Roman candles.
Running across the grass, fifty meters sometimes,
to where the ball had folded itself into the field. Swinging hard
back toward my house   as if it were a crowd
over and over. I wasn't training.
                         I didn't understand training.
     My swing—a dream stacking on others.
        Bottom of the ninth. Seventh game of the series.
          The World Series. Crack. Greatness.
        I'd tilt my cap, wave my hand.

It just comes down to physical ability, my dad explained—
a difference in upper body strength. Men. Women.
     My swing—a rubber band, expanding
        then snapping.

Snow day

Through the kitchen window, I watch you
shovelling what the plow left. You are talking
to the neighbour and I realize she is stunning.
But then, we don't have the same taste, do we?
The light in your eyes could melt the ice. The fairness
of your skin—your temperament. The fullness of your
sleeves, heavy snow and hearts and other cold things
scooped out from the bank, tossed over your shoulder.
You take care of things. Make things fly. You always have.
When you come inside, leave her scraping,
there is something I want to show you.

Homesick: Toronto

It's morning and too early—hungover,
hanging into this day from the last. Last night was fun
but I miss home. The city,
raunchy and decorated. Shine, sweat, dirt. Skin.
That's how it is on Friday, Saturday—
    I'd take a Monday, though.
The four of us hunched over the bar,
jeans and T-shirts draped just so off tired, thin bodies.
Everyone younger than they look,
much younger and worn—
worn in. It's harder than it looks—being a sissy.
Middle of the night till sunrise, bourbon on the back patio.
Spin the bottle. Slap or smack. Dare.
One more cigarette. Bitches—
these are the only men I've ever admired.

From God

Meeting you has been a gift from God, you say
and touch my arm for three long seconds.

Do you feel the same way now, flying
over the prairies? A half-empty
bottle of vodka staring at me from the table.

I'm fairly certain all the French you spoke
last night was filthy. Holiness, though,
as each word touched me, syllables
linger, tangled in the mess of this room.

Make no mistake, I wanted to kneel
before you. Make the glass shake. Fuck
you with my hands and mouth, a prayer.

February

I stayed up until two a.m. and let the taste
of vodka fill my mouth like wonder.
You, from the dark of our bedroom,
reminding me to take the dog out. My boots
damp from days of snow. Out into
the middle of night morning, snow light
reflected by low clouds, the glow
overwhelming the dark. Soft-edged
everything.
      The night listens as I try to explain
what's happened. The patterns
inside all these cold crystals melt
unnoticed. My jacket clotted with
wet sky, my cheeks red, everyone sleeping
except me and the dog, her nose pressed
into the blurry ground. I'm looking
at the sky, wonder pooled
under my tongue. Ringing light.

Lovers

When I write in the kitchen, I can see
through two windows into our living room
where you paint, sitting at the small drafting table
free to a good home—tossed into the back
of our truck. Most of your face is hidden
behind the sill. But the smooth of your cheek,
and the corner of your right eye, its tilt as you focus,
bent close to the page, betrays the wisdom
that wets your brushes and is so much—

Your handsome shyness. The constellations
of your wit. The curls that spill out of your hat,
woolen, the cotton of your sleeve. You dress
and undress me with your kindness. The way
your eyes see, the light they draw into my days
and on the page as you work—as we work—
gesturing, together and separately, saying
and unsaying.

Not knowing

We didn't know. You laugh at how often I say this,
but it fascinates me. You were there next to me
behind the counter. In aprons and plaids
and sneakers worn uneven from standing by the hot stove
in that bar, our bar. We sat through pints and endless
ounces of Wild Turkey. You listened to my stories,
your face warm and dimpled under
those lights so many times. We even fucked,
drunk and awkward the first time, guessing
who the other was, even though we should have trusted
the ways we fit together.

But we didn't know. On that patio, in the unfamiliar daylight,
is where it changed. You joined me for breakfast and
we talked until my evening shift. All I remember
is the story you told about the lesbian firefighter
in Argentina.
       That, and the way our bodies felt new on either side
of the table, where we had sat so many times before.

Faith

You can't drive through the snow if you don't trust. But
you can't relax either. Let your guard down. Have you ever
gone into a skid? Felt the heaviness of the car, how small
you are inside? Ever since I wound up in the ditch,
I have been afraid of the snow. Its soft disguise.
The way it turns the road into a cascade. Prayer
won't keep you on track. It's impossible
not to worry. The valley is close.

I always try to keep faith in my doubts, the Reverend Mother
says to Maria. This is the closest I've been to worship,
until now. I believe in carols, their music:
O, the rising of the sun, and the running of the deer.
You sounded free that night,
    calling me from the bookstore. Singing
Canadian poetry like psalms into the phone. Now I watch
from the couch as the von Trapp children sing, like larks,
to their father.

I woke up, sung a hymn to the Christmas tree: *Come thou
fount of every blessing*. Why is proof what we want?
Isn't a glimpse of divinity enough? I had never
been so hungry, but now without you on the other side
of these prayers, I'm too filled with grief to want. The quiet
is a breeding ground that asks what is the difference
between what you want and what you fear?

O, untouchable shape that greets me in the morning.
    Not yet awake,
slipping into you, and out again
    to the bright chill of my bedroom.
Your teeth on my chest. I was looking for God, but found you.
Are you cold? Let me warm you. I don't believe in anything
anymore, so please, please, please just speak
freely, like you did before.

Gestures

This Windsor knot secures nothing
but your glance. The delicate clip
on the edge of your stockings, you
are under my fingers on the leather
sofa. Around my fingers, you are
somewhere else with me—screaming back,
like the streetcars, at this Queen Street us.
And for these short weeks, I'll be the one
to unzip the back of your dress.
You'll pour the vodka and we'll fuck
the patriarchy with feminist fingers.
My watch near the frame of your glasses,
I brush strands of autumn from your face.
I catch my reflection in the lenses and see,
for a moment, the man you see.

Revelation

Like   revelation, when you got on top of me.
We reenact this moment for each other, sing hymns,
press palms together. The look on your face, the shift
of my abdomen above yours. The truth lurks—
in your looks to the sky, the birds circling
there, my head bowed towards
my water glass. I trace its translucent brim
with my eyes. The unbrokenness of some shapes,
the jagged edge of others. Mountains—
the tear they make in the blue of an almost-winter sky,
like this sadness in my tissue, hairline cracks in the
glowing yellow glass you blew over my skin. The screaming
your body puts into mine. I wake up with a quiet pain, but
don't close your mouth. Say my name again. My body
might just sprout wings and fly.

Cognition

Glancing at the lemon rind, soaked in vodka,
I take the nearly melted ice onto my tongue. You ask
me—and I'm not sure I can say.   I'm thinking
about how I forgot, in the fog of that morning, to tell you
how you looked in your dress, framed by birch.
I forgot to tell you how remarkable
in your grey T-shirt, tangled in bed sheets, you are—
the light of my dreams—glowing. The two of us
talk in the heat tossed off the stove. Your arm, its stirring.
Your mouth, its mischief.
    We draw out days with our repetitions.
Poetry. Tuning ears to bird songs. How perfect
the white-washed beams of the house.
    The matted gold grasses
brushing the limbs of the tide. Slips of paper, like birch bark,
stripped and added to kindling—strike anywhere—
the very air is flammable. But I'm hunched all the same
over the pieces of us, hands cupped, emptying my lungs
in steady gusts. Watching this orange seed dance,
curling the bark like your toes against the morning.
I am thinking about the inside of you. Perfect—
this couch and its whispers—
your feet in my hands
your feet in my hands.

Celebration

Ask me what I want to do today and I will answer
the same as always,   nothing really,
flip through the tarot deck
until we like what we see, sit with you
and feel your skin on my palms, wish
that you occasionally press your hands
against my shoulders, thighs, leave them there
for longer than I expect.

There are other things I want—
to catch all the water spilling
from the cups. No wonder
we have been pictured here
as birds. No wonder we have been
fishes too, in past lives: wings,
gills, webbing. Now
the only slimy thing is my heart,
the way it tries.

                    So just laugh
into the hotel sheets with me, it's my birthday,
or it might as well be. You're wearing nothing
but my shirt, your hair wet, the coffee pot whispering
our fortunes into the afternoon.

Girlhood

The motorcycle jacket my mom brought home from Denmark,
small enough for my niece now. Around the house mostly,
never to school. Cindy and I punching each other
on the hide—against our fists, the sound thick—
smoking too, in the backs of buildings   turning suburbs
into cities.   The summer   filling a ball cap
with water in the fountain, and tipping it
over our heads by the tennis courts. Baseball.
Alone in the field, hitting as far as I could,
then chasing the ball, out,
   way out, farther than I could hit now,
over and over—
            whatever it was is still there
            when I jump off the dock,
            one leg higher than the other, one hand in the air,
            the other on my nose.

Acknowledgements

Earlier versions of some of these poems first appeared in *Event, Prairie Fire, Grain, Canthius, The Puritan, Room, Poetry Is Dead, CV2, Plenitude,* and *The Stinging Fly*.

I would like to thank Leigh Nash, Julie Wilson, Megan Fildes, Andrew Faulkner, and the entire Invisible team. Working with you has been a joy. Thank you for believing in this book.

Thanks also to: Mr. Allen for fostering a love of poetry when I was in Grade Seven. The Banff Centre for supporting my work and the work of other artists—you are a treasure. The Beaver and everyone in it for being my queer lighthouse. Mella Brown for always being a willing reader when I need a tomboy second opinion. Colette Bryce for your attention to my poems. My family—Mom, Dad, Zebbie, and Gill—for your love and giving me an inflated sense of my abilities as a child. Tucker Finn for your bottomless love and encouragement. I miss you and your poetry.

Clare Goulet for teaching me so much about astonishment. Sue Goyette for your wisdom, poetry, and friendship, all of which have meant so much to me. Halifax Central Library, it's so comforting knowing that you're there. Erika Hennebury for shaping my early thinking about art making and helping me like olives. Corrina Keeling for making me gay. Annick MacAskill for your support and tireless work on this book, but most of all for the light you bring into my heart and poetry. Annika Mikkelsen for the good times. Will Munro for everything you made that held us all up, that held us all together. Adam Myatt